New Product Strategy in Small High Technology Firms

WORKING PAPER
ALFRED P. SLOAN SCHOOL OF MANAGEMENT

New Product Strategy
In Small High Technology Firms

Marc H. Meyer   April, 1983
Edward B. Roberts   WP# 1428-83

MASSACHUSETTS
INSTITUTE OF TECHNOLOGY
50 MEMORIAL DRIVE
CAMBRIDGE, MASSACHUSETTS 02139

New Product Strategy
In Small High Technology Firms

Marc H. Meyer
Edward B. Roberts

April, 1983
WP# 1428-83

NEW PRODUCT STRATEGY

IN SMALL HIGH TECHNOLOGY FIRMS

Marc H. Meyer and Edward B. Roberts
Sloan School of Management
Massachusetts Institute of Technology
Cambridge, MA 02139

OVERVIEW

This article presents an empirical method to examine new product strategy in small high technology firms. The purpose of this research is to determine the relationship between the degree of "newness" within a firm's portfolio of products, in terms of the embodied technology and market applications, and the firm's economic success. This concept of newness in the technological and market dimensions of new products represents the degree of "strategic focus" exhibited by the firm. Thus, this research is an empirical examination of the consequences of "strategic focus" in small high technology companies.

Research Background

Conceptual Framework

New product strategy requires a historical base for assessment. Only an understanding of past product activities can provide the full context by which to evaluate the challenges of new products. In turn, this comparison of the present to the past may be performed along two basic dimensions. The first is the newness of the technology within the new product relative to technology(ies) already developed by the firm. The second dimension is the newness of the

market application for which the new product is targeted compared with the users of past products. The pairing of embodied technology and market application for the examination of new product strategy is an idea used previously by many authors, including Johnson and Jones (1957)among the earliest, and more prominently by Rumelt (1972). Each of the two dimensions incorporates a set of factors For example, the degree of newness in market application includes levels of newness regarding product packaging, distribution channels, and support mechanisms. As each new product comes on stream, the cumulative body of the firm's technology and market experience grows accordingly, and is that much broader for the evaluation of the next new product effort. This dynamic framework is shown in Exhibit 1.

Within the technological dimension, the critical unit of analysis identified is the "key core technology(ies)" of a product. A core technology is a discrete, unique set of skills or techniques which finds application within a product or service. A given product embodies at least one identifiable core technology, and it may include several or more separate technologies. However, not all core technologies embodied within a product have the same impact upon the firm's competitive advantage. Accordingly, those particular core technologies which provide the firm with a proprietary, competitive edge and differentiate it from other companies making similar or substitute products have been identified as key core technologies [Ketteringham and White,1983]. Key core technologies can be distinguished from other technologies used by the firm that are commonly available in the marketplace as components. This latter, more broadly available group of core technologies are referred to as "base technologies". A high technology firm typically concentrates on a specific (or set of) key core technology, and by packaging or integrating it with a variety of component base technologies, generates its final product. The key core technology

EXHIBIT 1   THE PRODUCT INNOVATION GRID

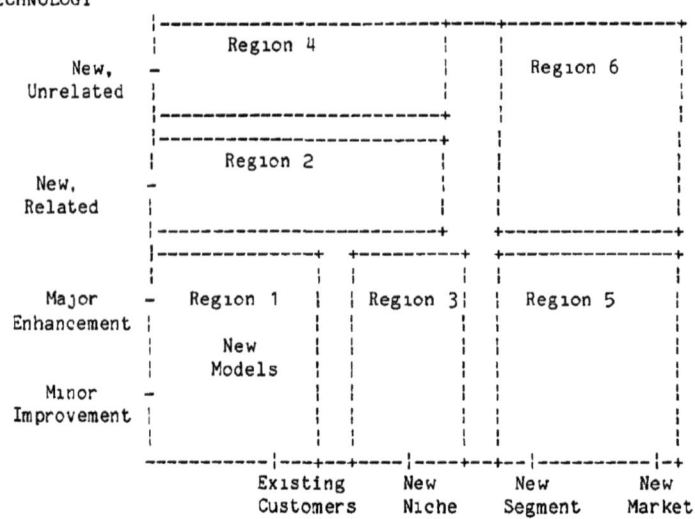

MARKET APPLICATIONS

becomes the basis for the "value added" of the firm. Clearly, this process occurs only in those firms that undertake their own product development and are not simply sales or support organizations.

Therefore, the differentiating element along the technological dimension of a firm's product portfolio is the degree to which each new product entails changes to the embodied key core technology of past products. This level of change runs along a continuous range of expended resources and effort. However, for the purposes of research, specific levels of change or newness can be identified.

The first two levels identified are "minor improvement" and "major enhancement" to a key core technology that the firm had developed some time in the past. Major enhancement is often achieved through the addition of new base technologies to a product line. By adding new components or subsystems, the firm can leverage its existing key technology into new product/market areas without having to develop additional new technologies of its own. The third level of technological newness is the development of a "new, related" key core technology, "related" by virtue of either sharing a product application in which the firm is presently involved or being combinable with an existing key technology into a wholly new product application. The development of a "new, but unrelated" key technology presents no such opportunity for combination with the firm's existing product technology. This is the last, and most extreme level of technological newness.

A schema for identifying levels of newness in the market application dimension, shown in Exhibit 2, has been adapted from the competitive structure model of Urban, Johnson, and Brudnick (1979). This model segments a market into a hierarchical tree structure by assigning possible product attributes to specific

EXHIBIT 2   COMPETITIVE MARKET STRUCTURE

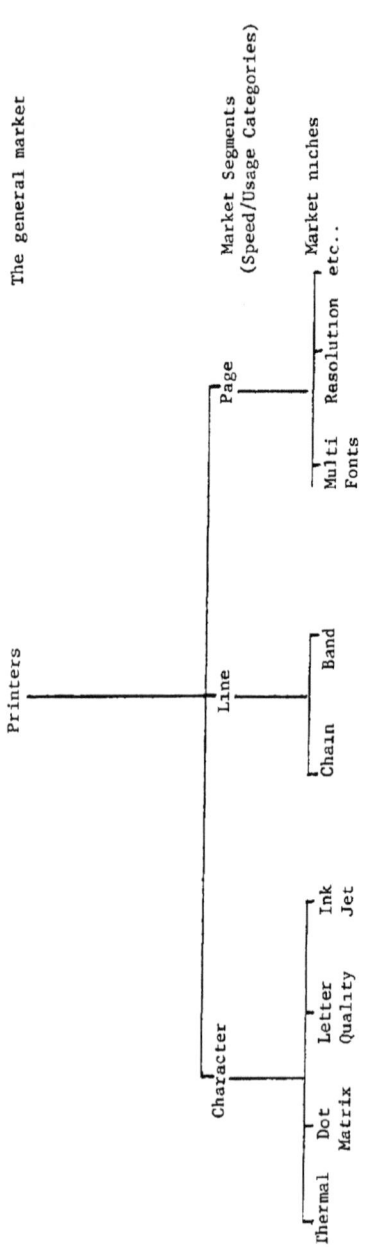

tree branches. These branches are defined by an analysis of the types and effects of product usage and the characteristics of users. Urban et al. show that the significance of individual tree branches can be established by measuring the probability of purchase under "forced choice" testing of consumers. In the adaptation of this model to the present research, the market tree structure(s) for a firm's products is derived by extensive discussion with the interviewees. However, individual tree branches are not statistically tested by random sampling of consumers of the firm's products. Additionally, the layers of the market structure are restricted to three generic levels: the general market, segments with the market, and niches within each segment. This taxonomy captures most of the degrees of newness in the target markets for new products. Since the market structures facing a firm can change over time, the degree of market newness assessed for a particular product is based on the "current" structure at the time of the new product's release. The market tree in Exhibit 2 was developed with the founder of a printer company that is part of the sample for this research.

The intersections of technological and market newness on the grid, sixteen in all, can be grouped into regions of new product activity. Region 1 of Exhibit 1 represents the release of new versions or models of current product lines, requiring some degree of enhancement to existing key core technology. In Region 2, the firm broadens its activities in an existing, or to a closely related, product/market by developing a new key technology that is combined in some fashion with the firm's existing technology. Forward integration would be an example of this type of new product activity. Region 3, on the other hand, is characterized by adaptive innovation. Here, the firm applies its existing technology to new sets of users who are closely related to current ones. In Region 4, a high degree of technological newness is combined with relatively low

market newness. This is a "customer-bound" focus where the firm tries to make markedly different products for a single set of customers. Region 5, on the other hand, represents extreme instances of adaptive innovation. Finally, new products that require the largest amounts of technical and market diversification fall within Region 6.

Hypothesis

The general purpose of the research is to examine the relationship between patterns of new product strategy and economic performance of the firm. The authors hypothesize that high technology firms which exhibit a high degree of strategic focus in their new product development activities are more successful than those which have less focus. In terms of the conceptual grid shown above, the authors hypothesized strong performance for those firms whose new product activities were minor improvement or major enhancement in the technological dimension, and were targeted for existing customers or new market niches.

The strategic direction suggested by the hypothesis runs counter to the tendency of American businesses to pursue diversity in their product technologies, as described by Rosenbloom and Abernathy [1982]. "Since the 1950s, a penchant for diversification has led U.S. firms away from their core technologies and markets." Part of the justification behind this asserted trend lies in corporate portfolio theory, which argues that overall risk can be minimized by having assets spread across a variety of product/market areas. Learning curve theory has also played a role in the tendency observed by Rosenbloom and Abernathy. By placing a high priority on major increases in manufacturing output to achieve economies of scale, management may forgo the flexibility needed to implement new, innovative features in existing product lines, a danger docu-

mented in the automobile industry by Abernathy and Wayne [1977]. Product development resources must, by default, be allocated primarily to other, newer business areas.

"Strategic focus", on the other hand, implies a level of concentration on a key technology area which, on average, may be the most important factor in the firm's effort to compete in the world marketplace. This source of competitive advantage seems even more critical for the particular type of company examined in this research: the small high technology firm.

The Sample

The framework described above was applied to a group of ten small high technology firms and their products, a subset of a larger sample developed for a multi-subject study on technological ventures. [Utterback, et al. 1982] That sample consisted of firms started between 1965 and 1975, incorporated in the state of Massachusetts, and whose main business involved the manufacture of computer hardware, e.g. whole computers, component boards, and peripheral devices. The products of these organizations are based on a relatively high degree of complex and changing technology. The ten firms used for the present research on product strategy were chosen by the convenience that the first author had carried out the original interviews with these firms and had access to them for follow-up data collection. The product-related sales of each of these ten firms for 1982 was less than $50 million.

Methods

Several criteria were imposed to determine what constituted a "product". The sample firm had to make each "product" with its own resources, either in

part or in whole, and commercialize the product under its own name at some point in time.   Consulting work, such as contract R&D, and projects which never resulted in released products were not included in the analysis; nor were "process improvements" which were not themselves marketed as products to the outside world.   Even though contract R&D and process improvements may play substantial roles in a firm's effort to generate revenues and search out new product opportunities, the problems of measuring them within the framework of new product strategy were prohibitive.

The extensive interview process, which, with one exception, was conducted with company founders, relied on a joint determination with interviewees of the levels of newness in both the technological and market dimensions contained in each new product in the respective firm's history.   This level of newness was measured relative to all product development activities undertaken by the firm prior to the specific release of a given product.   Therefore, the base against which both technological and market newness were determined grew with each successive product of a firm. The data were then plotted on a grid for each firm. A firm that had released ten products over the course of its history would have nine specific points placed appropriately on the grid (one for each product after the first).

The data were processed for analysis in three steps. First, each point on the grid was multiplied by a predetermined set of factors representing levels of technological and market newness. A variety of weighting scales were tested, with each set increasing by different margins for each level of newness (i.e. 1, 2, 3, 4 or 1, 3, 6, 10).   The results of the analysis proved insensitive to variations in the several scales tested.

The second step was to sum these multiplications for the entire grid of the

firm. Also added to this sum was the number of initial key core technologies
developed by the firm for its first product, multiplied by the weighting factor
for "new,but related" products   This addition accounted in part for those
firms which embark on ambitious startup projects.

The third and last step was to divide this total newness sum by the number
of points on the grid, e.g. the number of products which had been released by
the firm. This normalized the data for different numbers of products among the
firms, and produced the "product newness index" employed in subsequent analyses.

The operational hypothesis was that strategic focus, as indicated by low
product newness, would have a significant relationship with strong economic performance.   To test this hypothesis, a dependent variable representing growth
was required.   The one used for the research is based on annual sales, divided
by the age of the firm at each respective year of sales so as not to be biased
towards young, fast-growing firms.   It was not feasible to collect sales fig-
ures for every year of each company.   However, the past three years sales were
taken, and after dividing each yearly figure by the age of the firm at that
time, a mean was calculated. For example, the calculation for a ten year old
firm whose past three years sales were $4 million, $9 million, and $10 million
respectively would be $[(4/8 + 9/9 + 10/10)/ 3]$ or .83 . This serves as the meas-
ure of "growth" for the firm, in million dollars per year. Using this growth
variable, a broad range of "success" existed in the sample: some firms were
strong performers, while others were on the verge of bankruptcy.

Results and Discussion

The primary goal of the study was to develop and test an empirical

methodology, and not to generate predictive conclusions. A small sample was employed to that end. Nevertheless, the significance is high of the relationship between strategic focus, as measured by product newness, and growth.

This finding, which holds true for all sets of weighting factors, was tested for significance with Spearman's rho coefficient. The basic procedure is that the cases are first ranked according to the product newness index (in order of low to high) and then ranked a second time by the growth variable (from high to low). The sum of the squares of the differences for these two rankings is the basis for calculating the Spearman coefficient. Exhibit 3 illustrates the rankings and calculations for one of the weighting sets.

In testing for significance, the null hypothesis was that the predictor variable, product newness, would have statistically significant relationship to the ranking of the firms by commercial success. The alternative to this was indeed the main hypothesis of the study, that firms with strategic focus reflected in low product newness indices would tend to be strong performers, and those with greater diversity reflected in high product newness scores, poor performers.

The coefficient derived in Exhibit 3 is .89 . For a sample of size of ten firms, the coefficient would have to fall below .746 to be not significant at the .001 level (for a one-tail test). The significance of the findings was established by a comparable margin for each of the several sets of weighting factors employed in the analysis. Further, the method was applied to each dimension separately. The coefficient for the technological dimension was .70, which indicates a significant relationship at the .05 level. The relationship with strategic focus as measured by market newness only was even stronger, with a coefficient of .89.

EXHIBIT 3   NEWNESS PREDICTING GROWTH

Case	Main Product	Product Newness	Rank	Growth	Rank	d_1^2
3	Line Printers	2.75	1	2.73	1	0
2	Large Computers	2.80	2	1.96	2	0
9	Optical Character Reconition Systems	3.11	3	1.72	4	1
4	Portable Terminals	3.18	4	1.29	5	1
7	Perpheral Processors	3.29	5	1.85	3	4
5	Electronic Funds Transfer Terminals	3.57	6	.23	6	0
10	Microcomputer Systems	4.00	7	.01	10	9
8	Tape Calibration Devices	4.25	8	.11	7	1
1	Access Control Systems	4.38	9	.05	9	0
6	Speech Recognition Systems	5.25	10	.06	8	4

$$\text{Spearman's rho}(r_s) = 1 - \frac{6 \sum d_1^2}{n^3 - n} = 1 - \frac{6(20)}{990} = .89$$

* From Siegel (1956).

Discussion

These empirical results served as a foundation for further examination of the strategies of the ten firms and of the research methodology itself.

As stated above, the result of the analysis was that strategic focus as manifest in low levels of product newness had an observable relationship with economic performance. Firms that over the course of their evolution primarily remained in one key technology area for applications in familiar markets tended to outpace those which did not. Implied within this finding is that successful firms tended to choose a growth-sustaining core technology to begin their product development activities, thereby avoiding the high levels of product line diversity which would accompany a switch from an ill-fated technology to a new, more promising one.

The sample contained firms whose activities centered on a single core technology from startup to the present time, as well as companies which redirected their energies into new areas in order to remain in business. A descriptive portrait of a "good" initial key core technology which emerged from conversations with the entrepreneurs was that the technology should be challenging to implement, difficult enough so as to present a significant barrier to entry for would-be competitors. Also the key founders should have a clear perception or vision of how to achieve distinctive functionality in a sequence of future products utilizing the initial key technology.

More specific growth strategies were suggested from the interviews. One of these strategies was firms that developed products for new market segments or general markets were most successful if they leveraged their efforts on existing proprietary key technology. This may be accomplished by combining an existing

key technology with new types of components to generate the new product.

For example, in the sample were two firms which had each developed techno-logically similar desktop microcomputer systems. One of these companies was able to leverage its intelligent I/O controller board technology into the new product by purchasing or licensing all the necessary additional elements. This included the CPU, memory components, the Winchester disk, the CRT display, and the operating system which were assembled together with a specialized I/O con-troller board. The microcomputer was marketed a year and a half after its formal project initiation to systems integrators and software developers, many of whom were existing customers of the I/O controller board line.

The second firm, on the other hand, did not leverage its existing key tech-nology. Its main product was a line of magnetic tape head calibration instru-ments sold to computer manufacturers. Even though the firm acquired all the necessary hardware components from outside vendors, it chose to develop both its own proprietary operating system and a set of business applications packages. Additionally, the new product was targeted, rather unsuccessfully, for retail distribution. The level of diversity represented by the firm's actions was therefore high, falling in Region 6 in Exhibit 1 as compared to the Region 3 pursuits of the first firm described above.

A larger sample would provide the data required to better examine specific strategy alternatives. Further, although the analysis methods presented in this article produce a "focal point" of the firm's degree of focus, equally important insights may be found in the measurement of the variance around that focal point. Time dependent movement upon the grid is another possible technique for examining the strategy of the firm. Additionally, one might be interested in the portability of the authors' experimental results concerning strategic focus

and performance to larger firms. With these thoughts in mind, the framework and
methods presented here may serve as tools for continued research of new product
strategy in the high technology firm.

- 13 -

References

Johnson, S. and Jones,C. "How to Organize for New Products", **Harvard Business Review**, May/June 1957.

Rumelt, R. **Strategy, Structure, and Economic Performance**, Division of Research, Harvard Business School, Boston,MA, 1974.

Ketteringham, J. and White, J. "Making Technology for Business", in Lamb, R. **Latest Advances in Strategic Management**,(to be published) Prentice-Hall, Engle-wood Cliffs, NJ, 1983.

Urban, G. Johnson, P. and Brudnick, R. "Market Entry Strategy Formulation: A Hierarchical Model and Consumer Measurement Approach", Sloan School of Management, Cambridge, MA, 1979.

Rosenbloom, R. and Abernathy, W. "The Climate for Innovation in Industry: The Role of Management Attitudes and Practices in Consumer Electronics", Harvard Business School: 80-65, Cambridge, MA, January 1982.

Abernathy, W. and Wayne, K. "Limits to the Learning Curve", **Harvard Business Review**, Sep/Oct 1974.

Utterback, J. and Reitberger, G. "Technological and Industrial Innovation in Sweden: A Study of New Technology-Based Firms", Center for Policy Alternatives, Massachusetts Institute of Technology, WP 132-061A, Cambridge, MA, May 1982.

Siegel, S. **Nonparametric Statistics for the Behavioral Sciences**, McGraw Hill, New York, NY, 1956.

Lightning Source UK Ltd.
Milton Keynes UK
UKHW021247210119
335934UK00004B/343/P